GIFTS THE MOLE GAVE ME

Wendy Pratt was born in Scarborough, 1978, and now lives in Filey. She is a fully-qualified microbiologist, but also has a BA in English Literature, an MA in Creative Writing, and is working towards a PhD in poetry. She is the author of *Nan Hardwicke Turns into a Hare* (Prolebooks, 2011), *Museum Pieces* (Prolebooks, 2014) and *Lapstrake* (Flarestack, 2015). She can be found on Twitter @wondykitten.

Gifts the Mole Gave Me

Wendy Pratt

Valley Press

First published in 2017 by Valley Press
Woodend, The Crescent, Scarborough, YO11 2PW
www.valleypressuk.com

First edition, first printing (October 2017)

ISBN 978-1-908853-88-2
Cat. no. VP0105

A CIP record for this book is available from the British Library.

Cover illustration by Maxim Griffin.
Cover and text design by Jamie McGarry.
Edited by Martha Sprackland.

Printed and bound in Great Britain by
Imprint Digital, Upton Pyne, Exeter.

Contents

Acknowledgements

I would like to thank my husband for being the wonderful support he always has been; my publisher, Jamie McGarry for giving me a chance; and Martha Sprackland, whose careful, thorough editing suggestions helped bring the collection to life.

Some of these poems, or versions of these poems have featured in the following magazines, journals and anthologies: *The Valley Press Anthology of Yorkshire Poetry,* edited by Miles Salter and Oz Hardwick, *The Interpreters House, Prole, The Butcher's Dog, This Body I Live In*, an anthology edited by Kate Garret, *The High Window, Under the Radar, Clear Poetry, My Dear Watson*, edited by Rebecca Bilkau, *The Dawntreader, Rat's Ass Review, The Writing Motherhood Anthology,* edited by Carolyn Jess-Cook and *The Everyday Poet*, edited by Deborah Alma.

'A Northern Snow Scene' was commissioned as the Christmas message for Northern Soul. 'Amazing Grace' won first prize in the 2015 YorkMix competition.

for Matilda, always

If You Can Tame It, You Can Have It

Use a rod, and childhood as the bait,
tent the blankets of your youth, wait,
tap the fly across the bedding. Tickle chunky
teenage thighs and make them twitch. The knees
unshaved shapes you half remember,
the figure undefined by gender.

Use your fingers gently, no surprises,
whilst the twenty-year-old you is occupied.
Feel the lightness of her bones, the way
her insides loop around her spine, sublime.
Make her smaller. Push her under the bed, into a box
Swirl the bait, pull on the rod,

(the words are gathered underneath) and tap it lightly.
Make a come-hither movement. Drag it slightly
to the left, into your thirties. This time
be heavier of hand, be forceful but be kind.
Tap the lure across the objects in her room,
the things she keeps in her museum, her muse.

Get behind her at her desk, stroke her hair.
Dangle the fly across her forehead, tap it there
and there, on her fingers on the keys;
watch the letters turn back beneath.

In Search of the Perfect Purse

I want that purse you gave me
back when we were courting.
Even though I know it's downstairs
in the junk drawer, its broken-zipped
mouth gaping, still holding
the train tickets and Metro pass
from Paris, I want to own it again.

I want to find in it that picture you took
as we pulled out of the station, in which
my face is doughy with youth
and I have not yet learned
how to tame my hair. I want your hand

as we run up the stairs to our hotel room
in the attic, Klimt's *The Kiss*
over our bed like a blessing. I want
to put Paris back in my purse, that purse
I loved with its grown-up browns
and stitched gold and clasps and pockets.

I want to open that purse and find
the cardboard ticket from the Louvre
and the Pompidou and the receipt
from Le Refuge de Fondues where we
got drunk on red wine served
in baby's bottles and forgot to save
our wits for art. I want *that* purse.

No other purse compares.
This one has only room for my debit card,
the pale-faced photo that the clinic took
of you, the Post-it note you left me
on the Mars Bar that said in shaky capitals
'I LOVE YOU'.

Heart-Shaped Box

Bedroom-scape, curtain's end, she
picks locks, creases limbs, eyes
the world via MTV, folds herself from me.
Maths and French are tuned out like
lies. her language is low-groaned, a
shallow torrent as she grunges; plays Pisces
when it suits, fish-scaled and cool. When
she dreams of death, she can't comprehend – I
know she thinks of silk and black lipstick, and I am
at a loss, can't describe a head blown off. I'm weak,

can't tell her how empty suicide looks. I've
got Cobain on my lips, like spit, been
a bad mum, a tyrant, a jailer, locked
her in, rolled up her sleeves inside
out, and seen her superficial scars, listened to your
bleating, her bleeding out, her shallow heart.
She can't know how I shaped
her body, *in utero*, how she is a box
with my own heart in it, let loose in her for
years, watching black days turn to weeks.

Escherichia coli

after W.H. Auden

Always trust a microbiologist because they have the best chance of predicting when the world will end.
– Teddie O. Rahube (Microbiologist)

My darlings, I have kept you warm
  for one day and one whole night.
I've kept you dark, and seen you're safe,
  and now I take your plastic
universe, the cosmic sheen
  of condensation falling
from the lid, and raise up the roof
  of your world so I may see.

You have been spoilt. You have dined out
  on sheep-blood and soy digest;
lived your lives in all-inclusive
  exclusivity. Your sun
has been the dome of a heat lamp,
  your beaches salted with eight
percent sodium chloride, you
  have had a good long summer.

Grow, my little ones, grow out
  across the red sheen, expand
your single cells into the bright
  wheels of yellow colonies,
pit the plate in your rush and run
  the great race to the edge
of your world. And find that there is
  nothing more. I will provide more.

Tomorrow I'll lift a select
few from your earth. It will be
your Rapture. You will ascend
and be baptised in sterile
H_2O. A bijou bottle
will be an ocean of tears
for you. Hold on, you are going
to a better place. Hold hands,

entwine flagella. You must face
apocalypse. You can not
know who will survive, who will die,
how the antibiotic
discs will decimate your numbers;
will dissolve through the agar
that you're living on, will force
upon you infertility,

a weak cell wall, metabolic
incompatibility,
death. I would like to think your lives
were not unbearable. You
have come from very distant lands,
explorers from the bland bowels
of some old lady, of some small
and helpless child. I needed

the knowledge of your deaths to send
back to your homeland. I am
a cruel deity. I have played
your hand for you, have ordered
every second of your free will.
Forgive me. When I am gone,
I will bequeath myself to you,
and your faith will be renewed.

Heading Home from Market Weighton

Early doors: the sun a hard rind
over the tops, fog sleeping in dips
across the road. I've left him,
forlorn, in a new job he hates;
suddenly my son instead
of my husband. I'm too near home
to turn back. The lies I told
to get him through the day are
already mildewed. The umber tail
of a fox beneath a hedge is absolute colour.
White lines peel under the wheels,
catching on the hours still to come
and somewhere, back there, his day
is being metered out in misery.
When I return, our home feels hot
and bruised beneath my palm.

Amazing Grace

Here is the divide: here
the pregnant wife, here
the grieving mother.
And in between,
a father, a husband, a man in a vacuum
as the surgeons run past.

After the sudden hydraulic drop
when time of death is called
the woman will emerge,
a sleeping Cleopatra on a white barge.

That little thing lost between pregnancy and birth
is a sinkhole beneath them,
sudden and inexplicable.
And don't they look uncomfortable
for the photos? Their unnatural smiles, their heads
flicking back and forth, knowing that these
are the only images they'll have.

Like shuffling cards, those emotions.
Then here, at three a.m., where halogen
anoints her husband on the camp bed,
she lies on her side staring at her daughter
and wonders how she can feel so lost,
but yet so found.

Macey Draws

She uses stencils to draw rounds,
tucks sounds into these pictures,
lays pencil borders round and about.

In her world fire is flat, a roundabout;
a circle with a centre. Flowers turn in rounds
over and over, the same design. Her pictures

are bird seed on her path. Those pictures;
one day I'll try and show her what it is about,
how fire takes hold in the soul and does the rounds,

half burns you away, curling the edges of your pictures.

Washing Up

Somehow, she couldn't tell you
when, she'd made a family
from paper dolls and furnished
a home with paint-on love.

Then, when the gas-man laid
a hand across her back, that day,
it cracked a white light through her,
numbing her hands. She watched

their rhythm in the water
and the way the suds made a milk-white
foam across her wrist, and had to ask

again and again and again if the dishes
she was washing were dirty or clean.

Danse Macabre

You wear your death like dance slippers,
taking them out of their coffin-box
at the barre. You *arabesque* and *plié,*
allegro lightly round the room, touch the mirror,
turn, feel your feet bleed into the blocks,
assemblé on your own edge, bitter

and full of remorse. The dance becomes a quickstep,
a flamenco, a stream of soft tap, a foxtrot.
The slippers lead. But you are no black swan.
Someone needs to stop you and pull you back, help,
step quicker.

Dreaming in Lithium

Salar de Uyuni where lithium gathers,
embroidered through the gummed edge
of the salt flat, the baked bowl
where Tezcatlipoca lounges,
yawning time into the stars.

Here lithium is frantic; it casts about,
searches for substance, skittering
between states, its little sun-god
desperate to be alight.

Powdered to a small pill it is
a bomb that will split the salt
from my core, realign my current
without the need of temple pads,
white nightgowns. Back in Uyuni

the dogs bark madly, mud huts stutter
on the faltering skyline, the Milky Way
is merged to the ground, changes places.
The sun opens a bright eye behind my lids.

With thanks to Lawrence Wright, whose article
in the New Yorker, 'Lithium Dreams', written
about the lithium mines at Salar de Uyuni,
inspired this poem.

In Scarborough

In Scarborough there's a grey seal
out at sea, a stack of dripping lobster pots,
a whelk seller wearing a woolly hat,
a nostalgia of postcards in a white rack.

The view is inside out with cold.
There is *In memory of* and *who loved to sit here*
or *came to Scarborough every year.* There's a wind
that whips grass on the headlands, hats are lost here.

In Scarborough the word is *funicular.*
There's a fuss and fluster as the season starts.
We've been huddled as gulls while the North
has been shut down. Now someone's fed the meter

and we can all begin again. There's a curve
to the Valley Bridge suicide rail, there to keep us safe
from ourselves. We jump, in Scarborough,
with the sea in our face. In Scarborough

there was a statue of Richard III, last king to reside
in our sea-scathed castle. There's an empty cage
where we thought we'd kept our history safe,
there's a space where he was, but it's been scrubbed clean.

Dry Stone Walling

This lane is tapping its teeth
in frustration, desperate
to speak to me about gorse and sheep.

It voices the stone walls into strata layers,
as if an earthquake has ruffled them together.
Sometimes they are sliding off the end,

a cramped writing hand
patted into place with all the knacks
and ticks of language. I can see the sly sling

of a too small rock behind the curve
of a shoulder blade. I can see the lift
and wedge and lift and wedge,

the voices raised on either side,
the Friday night pint, the church days,
the wages wedged in an old tea tin.

The valley darkens,
Stories are left alongside the tools,
sticking like cement between the gaps.

What Dreams May Come

I

In the dog days the sun stays late,
whisks horizons to egg white peaks,
heats the air to an opiate beat,
heavy in the fibrous night.

II

Dropping down the stoop
into an un-tongued terror, the clench
against the dark; waking, lifting your body
up out of a bubbling wreck,
breath gone into a warren of small gasps.

III

Dank and heavy as a wet hem, the night
steals sleep, measures breath
in a squeeze-box routine
of sticky lungs, swollen tongues.

IV

Jolt. A child, terraced
and far away, cries a riddle of screams
to its mother. A car lights the room,
teeth chatter to a rattle in your head.

V

A sudden burst of drums,
a guitar being tuned, you wake
and settle your ears to the night,
listen for the seagulls like papercuts in the black.

VI

Something deeper: Venice,
a hotel balcony, a sparrow eating crumbs.
A car below blows its horn,
two lovers are fucking on the lawn.

VII

You watch the blinds drip
in the humidity. You wait
for thunder, a strip light to clean out
the crags and crannies, the damp corners.

VIII

Dawn muses the cat to the sill, jackdaws
croak in the guttering, seagulls rail
against the songbirds. A breeze
lifts the blind, just slightly, just.

The Art of Breaking Glass

There is an art to breaking glass,
a skill in all the panes I've smashed.

There is a skill to snapping stems,
an art to chipping off the ends

of ornaments; Murano fish,
a skill within the crackled dish.

There's skill in scattering the bits,
a thrill in V-shaped finger nicks.

And every time I fall through one
I can't resist the siren's song.

I've fallen straight through full-sized doors,
I've stamped my feet on thick glass floors.

I've ground my heel on sea-glass pieces
picked from crevices on beaches,

picked up broken bottle-necks
and pressed them up against my flesh.

I even have a box at home
containing fibreglass, like foam.

I fell through my first pane in a faint,
head bowed divinely like a saint,

I never felt the slightest pain,
so I performed the act again

and I've been falling ever since
to somehow prove that I exist.

Now the Wolf is in the Cul-de-sac

it's come down with the dusk, left
a vast geometry of pines, thin lines
of Christmas trees, sheep hemmed
into grey-black fields. It's worked
its way along the red brick walls,
PVC doors, nudged wind chimes
with its nose, paced the patios
and blanched itself to white in each
security light. You watch it coming,
your hands, like X-rays on the glass,
your face as undone
as an Etch A Sketch, and all
that keeps the wolf away is light.

So each house lights its windows;
kitchens guillotined to squares,
bathrooms' petalled fingerprints
of oblique headshots over sinks.
The wolf leans up against
your letterbox and presses
forward with the wind, and unlike
the house dog on the sofa,
wolf knows neither sit nor stay.

Starlings

When my mum returns
to her kith and her kin
she becomes a starling
on a wire. Gathered for flight
with her sisters, tweezer-beaks
snip-snip together, oil-spill
backs meet and merge
in speckled readiness.
Yellow legs no more
than matchsticks grasp
at brandy and lemonade
or gin and tonic, tiny hooks
tap-tapping on the smooth curve
of glass. Then a sudden bloom into flight.
A murmuration, they twist
and plait together, stubs
of wings frantic, lifting up
above Thirsk town; the cobbled
market square, The Golden Fleece,
the picture house still echoing the sounds
of stamping cowboy feet. Up higher,
the Hambleton Hills become
an ordinance survey map, Sutton Bank
a rind or a lip, the White Horse of Kilburn
a child's chalk drawing. They rise, away
from the roaring and gurning of hungry bairns,
the bad 'uns in queer streets, the bonny lasses,
canny lads, me mam and her sisters. They are calling
for her sharp, short *Look! Look!*
Here's our Eilee, here's our Eilee, now then
now then now then.

Heptonstall Graveyard

God, the wind. It peeled the stones
from the skull of St Thomas' church,
left its mouth slacked to a yawn or a scream,
sounding vowels through the nave, through
the clock-eye, the altar stones, the flat-backed
flat-packed dead in their wedding gowns.

I couldn't have placed you here, in this wind.
You are not even in the gothic ruin, where you might
have met your curse head on, but in the bleak
modern field where the new builds' bathrooms
back onto you, and children squeal on trampolines.

They have bitten a hole in the ground
for you, and mouthed you into the soil,
smaller than the giant I'd imagined,
with both your surnames finally intact.
You're sandblasted by the wind,
here where nothing grows
and the votives left to you cling
like limpets in your dark.

Pluviophile

When it comes, thick and soft
as the pelt of an animal,
I am grounded, brought down
to calm in the smell of damp earth.
We wait like the wet starlings
under tree cover, their song-work
undone in the shallow hiss
of leaves and rain. I am paused,
smelling the green of the grass,
the hung heads of daffodils,
watching the plough-furrows
fill with water. A dog barks
somewhere, on one of the farms,
and the spaniel lifts his wet head, waits
as I wait – we are communed,
marooned, standing peacefully,
watching the water make mud
out of soil, movement out of stillness.

Gifts the Mole Gave Me

My own face staring down,
the arc of a horizon
framing my head
like a portrait. The world
staggering backward behind me,
the dog curved to a streak
on the convex mole-eye.

The memory of sleep,
the plush of a velvet heart,
the scraping away, day
after day, enough soil
to glob a mouth shut,
shut a world in,
pick treasures out.

Picking Mushrooms

Crows take flight, slide onto the dawn
with a rasp. They are the loose shale of the woods.

There are three miles of trees and dry stone walls
that bristle in the grass, and at my hip, bay bolete,

birch polypore, field blewit, chanterelle,
horse fungus. Lifted gently, fingers hooked

beneath their gentle heads, touching the secret skin
of their gills, I pick and pick again. I am a reaper

and I lay them out on my cool kitchen marble,
counting their pale limbs into my red pan.

Fallen Sheep

The nostrils warm a melt-circle
across her chin and hinged-lid mouth,
slack, with a higgle of old headstones,
her tongue a lazy slide of spit.

The balsa-thin skull might yet be found,
still attached to a spine, as spring
arrives with an archaeology of death,
when all the white gives way to colour.

Once, I passed a nursing home while walking.
I saw a woman lain this way, a cartouche of decay
through an open door. She was half out
of an easy chair, the woven armrest
wet with spittle; her grunting breath, the teeth,

her white nightdress hitched above one knee,
the pale November light packed all around her.
They came, those smiling nurses, dressed in blue,
and hoisted Lottie to her feet.

She let them pull and push her
until she was upright, stunned;
feeling misplaced in a different light.

Barbara's Farm

Where the house gapes
into the road, spring petals
have lodged on the sill.

There was always a deep dung smell,
shaggy black heads hanging over a rail,
a shuffle of feed in a bucket. A 'come by
come by come by' from my dad.

The moon lights her face through the ceiling,
as she sleeps in her hat and her gloves,
and the farm falls in chunks to the street.

The wind is picking the roof over,
letting jackdaws down into the chimney,
the eaves have gone to seed, and I have blown
like a dandelion head, a burst of flies,
come by come by come by.

This is Where We Nearly Died

One lady clutched her novel
like a crucifix, the men shrugged on
their nonchalance, a mother and her child
became religious art. There was a whir

of static from the cockpit. The cabin crew
behind the curtain like a Punch and Judy show
stayed silent, waiting for their cue.

They don't tell you, on the plastic sheet,
when to say *I love you.*

Directions

I

First, lope through the white tumble
of cottages; woodsmoke lazing
along the roofs, still leaves
burning the sky. The dog
will see a squirrel, a sharp, grey
beat of life among the silence.

II

Turn sharp into Back Lane, follow
the course of a stream that will meet
the Hertford in its time. For now
it is younger than that fat, old tongue
of river, with a voice
like glass being shattered.

III

Stop at the corner of the mushroom farm.
See what entwines in the ditch;
a hawthorn leans, exhausted, a fence
beam grappling at its roots. Still the red
berries bleed against the cold, the branches
bold-black, the ivy like a rash.

IV

Into the field, turn a right angle,
face the ancient quarries on the side
of the dale. Look down, search
for arrowheads, pottery, a word
or two on the edge of some chipped
rim that says that someone else
once lived. Observe the molehills.

V

Now down the chalk path rolling
on to Lingholme Farm. Here
is where the Star Carr people's lake
met its dry edge. Here is where
the water drained away
and now the courtyard
waits for the next ice age.

VI

Round the curve to the crossing;
high hedges, bleached-red farm
equipment waiting in the stubble
of cornfields. The barn owl drops
its wings to the dawn. It has left
a pellet on a dry stone wall; a leg
bone, a skull cap of fur, something
like a claw.

VII

Turn again at the horse chestnut tree,
poke a toe and search for conkers
in the burnt sienna leaves. None.
Inhale the sea on the breeze.

VIII

Head up the hill and back towards
the village. Look over the landscape,
look for tumuli, look for signs
of the Viking settlement
that gave this place its name. Look
along the field edge for roots.
Let the dog dip into the stream.
Follow the path right round, look for hares.
Listen to the sound of something small
making its way underground.

Chapel

Jesus lived behind the organ,
beneath the curved struts
of a whale's ribcage.

Sundays were a whine of hearing aids,
a stumble of walking sticks,
special cushions brought from home.

The radiators could burn a knee
or a hand. The organ player watched
through the rearview mirror.

There was a fine line between
church-smart and slutty. Jesus watched
from the wall above a storage box.

There was a marble wedged in a gap
between the floorboards. Noah and Jonah
were best, because of all the animals.

The preacher's room was a musk of dust,
with a black muffled safe. The collection
was counted behind frosted glass.

Harvest festival was a giant bread loaf,
Easter was a cross made of flowers,
Christmas was a burning orange.

The orange squash was flavoured water,
the teapot was the colour of post-war Britain.
There was interminable chatter about illness.

My first communion was a disc of nothing,
a tiny beaker of juice, a stutter of words,
a disappointment with transubstantiation.

October was my dad standing on my dress,
flowers round the church door, everyone
smiling and crying, fervent vows.

It was a lack of answers. It was convenient
answers. It was a decision not to take
communion again. It was frowns, nudges.

Mother's Day was a posy of daffodils,
it was my mum saying I could have hers
when they missed me out, it was awkwardness,

it was me parting the sea of faces, like Moses,
people saying our prayers would be answered,
it was knowing I couldn't pray because I didn't believe.

It was the shadow of Jesus turning out to be
nothing more than a stack of chairs
in the storage space behind the organ.

Down Sutton Bank

Pine trees
dusty and silent, the gap
between each row widening
and narrowing
like the beam of a lighthouse,
the thought of Bigfoot
crossing slope-backed, staring you down
as you sat in the back seat. An open field,
dry stone walls, well kept.
Sheep, moors, dales, a spine of pale white stones,
a peaty dark of standing water,
a golden puddle of sunset.
On the edge, like a signal station,
the visitors' centre, a brown
disabled-toilet door, a car park of grinding
gravel, tufted grass, the prehistoric
green of fern, the Scots pine fringe,
a red triangle of descent: 25%.
Chalk bones. A lurch, a feeling of being
in a lift, of falling forward.
A steady drone of brakes.

You are eye-level with the wall, the ground. Your dad
points out your great auntie's house, slap-bang
in the middle of the hill. The memory
of a family party, smoking
with your cousins in the dark, the bright flint
of a lighter, low voices, an uncle close by
asking *where's the bairns?*
Music, a constant stream
of car lights winding. Now
I can't find the gate, can't work out how
we drove up – like an Escher drawing, it seems
unfindable. And she doesn't live there anymore.

Portrait of St Francis of Assisi in the Bath

There is steam, and a slant
of winter light on opaque glass,
the sound of wood being chopped
down in the village. The cat's back
is glittering with condensation.

When you lean out of frame
to wash your hair, the beige tiles
miss your profile. When you bend
to dip your head, your return
is a miracle.

Your hands are cupped to the cat,
he laps, eyes closed.

You turn towards me, knowing
I was watching all along. You are radiant
in this moment. A sparrow
lands on the sill, shrills twice,
we turn our heads in unison.

A Northern Snow Scene

All the kids are out today, and sometimes a dog
chases his pack down the hill, and sometimes
someone's mam shouts from the ember of a doorway,
so that every head turns to see whose tea is ready,
who's going for their bath and who will dare stay out
till the wide sky, leaning on the slope's top edge,
tows the silhouettes of trees down to their shadows.

Night Windows

Edward Hopper, 1928, oil on canvas

There is too much heat
in New York. Too much heat
in the hotel room, in the frame
of the open window,
in the unnecessary radiator.
There is too much heat in the blaze
of a single bulb, too much heat
in chafed thighs, in cleavage, in armpits,
in neck creases, in the squinting
eye of a belly button.
The silk tags on sweat, rides up
as she bends and packs or unpacks
unwanted clothes. The night
is a dozen things on a list,
a number on the back of a receipt;
ink smudged in the heat.

Advice on Marriage

For Amy and Matt

Let love be your guide-rope.
Let the lines on your palms
be your map. Let the heat
of a held hand be a homing
beacon; the lightest fingertip-
touch on the hip or the waist;
let this be your lifejacket.

Let Groupon vouchers
for afternoon tea be a currency
in your own personal country.
Let ten minutes together at six a.m.
be as precious as a lifetime's love.
Don't be afraid to reopen old wounds,
you are each other's blood brother now.

When a storm comes, or a swell
of worry, let the gold band
on your finger be a life ring,
let your marriage be your raft.
Be each other's shelter; no structure
is stronger than two people in love.

Capture today and the days to come,
press them like flowers,
make a watermark on both your hearts.
Fill all four chambers with today and roam
the memory. Revisit it a hundred times,
touch it like Braille, read it like scripture,
feel the weight of it, like the touch
of a kiss on the cheek, like the click
of consonants and the soft roll of vowels
as they slip over your lips, as you utter *I do*.

25 Hibernia Street

Where we first found ground,
cooled our feet, hot from running
through our wedding vows.
The building still craved your ex,
was still giddy with her palette.
I found her hair in the bell jar
of the Dyson, saw her shadow
smeared, on the carpet,
brushed her fingers off the rim of the bath,
her sweat from your back. We nibbled
the walls down to horsehair and lime,
took a hammer to the kitchen tiles.
I felt for a pulse in the cornicing, listened
at light fittings for the house to heave
a cellarful of dusty air. We applied
a cool flannel of fresh plaster, the calm
of neutral colours. And in its skeletal state
it accepted; it smoothed its walls for us,
weakly offered up rooms for our use,
let us place our wedding photo,
like a tattoo, on the pale cream of the hall.

Half Empty

The pub is heaving, the party poppers popped,
the several-gin-and-tonic-touchy-feely crowd
have swallowed up your peace. Your corner
oozes negatives. Like a wrongly placed decimal point
your face refuses to register.

They label you a miserable old fool, a miser,
a scrooge, a fundamental mental case,
a billy-no-mates, and they party out the party.

But you stay for hours more, exuding anger,
scowling at lovers and drunks, because at least
it feels like being alive, and anger is so close to love.
Then you sip your bitter bitter and go home.

Unconditional

for Sandy

Here lies your body, curled
beneath the old pear tree,
separated from your pack.
Here, more than twenty years
ago, aged twelve, I sat and taught you
stay and sit, shared bonemeal biscuits
with your gentle mouth and twirled
the whorl of fur that made an eddy on your chest.

Your ribs a ridge I stroked in evenings
by the fire, your body my pillow
through the TV years, your ears
an idle plaything while I read, or wrote,
and passed away our time.
I missed your death.
I missed the last years of your life,
my gentle boy. I left you

on your own. I wonder if you wondered
where I'd gone and why I'd left
to live with someone else.
Did you listen for my footfall,
head on paw, or cock your ears,
or raise your nose, remembering my smell?
I was only a mile or two away,
and could have stroked you more,

or called to throw a ball
for old time's sake. Or sat with you,
grey-muzzled on my lap, and let you lick
my feet, and stroked your back.
Here lies your body, curled
beneath the old pear tree.
For twenty years we kept your collar,
like a promise, in the kitchen drawer.

Godsong

Lose the trail of prayers that hang
about the head like moths and watch,
instead, the tendon of road swerving
through a bluster of trees.

Birds will fall away, losing their song
to your footfall as you ignite
the leaves as only you can; bleed
into the heat beneath your feet.

Swing to the rhythm; you are sudden
and serene at once. Your heart is a fist,
clenched, remembering what it is
to survive, not just exist.

Stepping into My Own Footprints

18th April, I am making green tea
and toast when the ghost of myself
arrives in the kitchen, bump first.
She sports the plastic bangles

and greasy hair of a two-day hospital
stay, and drifts past me, unwilling
to register that a future me can exist.
There is nothing but her moment.

They have sent me home and told me
all is well. Already I am laying
down footprints to fall back into, year
after year. The last echoes of those failing

kicks will stick to my feet.
My baby's birthday is always fresh snow,
masking the normality of kettles
and toasters, things that take the same shape

in the same places each year; the drowned
steeples of our snowed-in world. Each year
my footprints wait for a new me to know
their shape, where the old snow is smothered,

smoothed. There is a permanent trail
of anniversaries, and my fingers are blue
from rooting beneath the white.

Hay (Na) Ku for Mirtazipine

sleep
comes in
great black waves

I
am washed
like beach pebbles

groggy
and emptied
I am shelled

I
am unstuck
from my bones

sleep
comes with
great black dreams

I
am drying
in paler light

sleep
comes still
is incessant

I
am salted
like dead fish

sleep
comes softly
a cat's paw

I
am waking
I have woken

Heart /Tide

In the dark, a tide pulls blood
through the needle-eye
of a heart valve, blueing the skin
from beneath. We are nothing but fluid.
Draping ourselves along the tideline
of our lives, meeting and receding,
spreading thin as lace across the sand.

And underneath, the silky plush
of blood sucking through the caverns,
the clinging vine of veins
and arteries. Lie down, lie still on the beach
and feel the pull of the moon in your blood,
feel the barrier of your skin, a thin sheen
keeping one tide out, one tide in.

Holbeck Hall Hotel

There is grass sliding in scales,
a bottle of expensive whisky rolling
into the dense earth like an offering.

Hold up a hand to block the kindling stack
and see the trick: a man smoking
a cigarette, a woman bobbing down
the steps, a car parked on the curved drive,
filled with luggage. The Janus house smiles,
still. It is in denial. This hazy-warm day,

the speedboats and sailboats skipping over
slight waves, the arcades singing, these things
aren't changed. The marble fireplace cracks
in two. A dollhouse wall is removed, the intimacy
of a bedroom flashed open. A jacket still hangs

on the door peg. The crowd eat ice cream,
dog-walkers stop. The hotel tears a hundred
years of parties, weddings and weekend breaks
to confetti, pushes its oak panelling into the sea.
The audience hums their satisfaction.

Interdependency

Here is the water: a swift kiss, a curlew
touching beak to foam, beak to foam.

A sandpiper, a seagull hung like an effigy
and gone. The cool black stones under my toes,

the sharp small shells, the pain that is a pleasure;
the sharp, sand-cracked, hard-soled pain,

a sandpiper's drill, insignificant.
Here is the softer, wetter sand. Here

is the cool floating debris, the seaweed,
the small white horses falling at my feet.

The world is curved here and the light
so bright it hurts and forces my hand,

like a captain, to see the sweating line
of the horizon. There is nothing between it

and I. My atoms make up the sand and the sand
is made from the stars that made the earth. I am

the horizon. I am the water, the oxygen, the air.
I am that boat; a black pixel on a blue screen,

I am the iron in the stone, the coral and the curve
of the seashell is my collarbone

The scaffold holds me,
pins the horizon, pulls in the sea.

Dog Walk on Christmas Day

First light, there is the sunrise,
warming to colour in the grey lane.
And my dog knows
no difference between this day
and any other. The sheep rumble
in their woolly world, or lie
like granite ghosts along the hedgerows.

On Main Street the delicate magic
of Christmas lights blink,
the village Christmas tree
bows gently in the breeze. The pub
and church are sleeping still,
but some houses are waking,
some children are up, parents
bleary, bolstered by coffee.

Other dog-walkers raise a gloved hand,
touch their hats, smile and wish
the Christmas day upon us.
Goodwill passed hand to hand in relay.

This morning I will pass the baton on,
in the lane, in the village, in my home,
where we enter the mulled warm
of heating, warmth, and light.

Encore

You come back with the cliché:
the final act repeated, the belongings
packed and unpacked, the sky ripped up
then patched up in the sober light,
each time another sliver off your life,
counted out in guilt.

One day that bungee-rope –
umbilicus to hope – will snap
and all your bones
shudder to a stop.
We'll know then that it wasn't
a game after all. Or

we'll know nothing of the sort;
bear witness to a badly acted
scene in which the heroine
steps off the stage, clumsily,
bruising the audience below,
who are gaping up, slack-jawed, denied
the final word.

Fear of Open Spaces

It's not the spaces that you fear,
it's the faces, the fish eyes
and sour breath or worse,
that buttery, rancid tang of decay.

It's not the park or the beach, the fear,
it's the supermarket, the town centre
and the people pressing up against you
like salmon, and the fear of learning to talk

without curling your lip.
And when you get inside, behind
the glass, the door closes
over your head like mud,

sealing you in,
making a fossil of you.

I Wear My Madness Like a Locket

At least three times in any year
I lift it from its welt, burn
the thin skin off its edges
like dried paint, so I can dredge

its dark centre, split its hinged
rim to see inside. Eye-thing,
rolling wildly in its socket,
it looks back, a kaleidoscopic

kit with many pieces and sets.
Sometimes it almost isn't there.
Sometimes the locket swings
happily and gifts me weeks

of non-stop work, and I feel
godsent. But the wheel
inside the case turns
without my knowledge,

pushes hurt into my chest like a stake.
I am left looking into it,
making monsters from its flame-shadows,
the world outside all aglow.

Locking the Cock-Birds Up

This is the love time for cockerels.
They strut up against the fence,
mighty in their miniature society.

At dawn the cockerels catch the sun in their beaks.
Like triggered traps their heads snap back.
Small throats expand, pour the sound out to the sky.

Yesterday, the sly-shuffling neighbour-birds
complained. A letter came. The rod-backed
council-bird decided my cockerels were loud.

I cloaked them with a black sheet,
in a box in the shed, and made their night
twice as long. Now I play God

with their world. Now they don't know
the earth and don't know the sun
and don't know to be sad about it.

Jesus Heals the Blind Bullshitter

The third time I catch him,
drag his skinny arse down Brid high street,
spitting to the wind,
seeing his stubble rubbing her saggy
breasts each time I close my eyes.
We get to the shop with its bleeding heart
flashing on and off, and there's the man
himself – feet up, floating above his desk.
I drag Bullshitter in. *SIT.* Bullshitter sits.

Jesus says *Now then*, or *Ey up*
but with a public-school accent
and it grates a bit. I slap twenty
down. *This one is blind*, I say.
Jesus spits into his hand, wipes
the glob of Holy Sputum across
Bullshitter's lids. *See, my child.*
And Bullshitter leaps up, *Fuck me!*
I see men walking like trees!

Jesus blushes. *Doesn't always work*
first time, sorry. I take ten of the twenty
back. Jesus wipes Bullshitter's eyes
again. There's a pause. I can see
that Bullshitter knows what he's done
to me, how he's been a twat. He half kneels,
half clasps his hands in prayer: *I love you*
for your body, but I fuck her for her mind.
Suddenly, the scales fall from my eyes.

Piano Lesson No. 3

The saints are not marching in.
They are dragging slow, painful
feet across the keys, bludgeoned
by the rhythm. When the waltz
starts up it doesn't skip, instead
it leans, drunk, between one timing
and another. And the reggae beat
which I worked at all week: stoned
and slatternly. The right hand catches up
to the left too fast, the syncopation lost
in a flurry of panic. At home I wait until
everyone is out, sit down at the walnut
blaze of afternoon-sunlit-piano and beg
my fingers to be polite, act well. They don't
listen, they're singing to their own tune,
racing ahead to Chopin and Nymen,
throwing scales to the wind in their hurry.

Sixth Birthday

You would still be small enough
to pull onto my knee; a kindling
of hot, slim limbs, your shape
not quite removed from babyhood.

I would brush sand from the soles
of your feet, rub the salt
from your shins with a towel, try
to hold on to this seaside-smiles girl.

Maybe ice cream – a hot fudge sundae
at the Harbour Bar. Your heart-shaped face,
and mine, reflected in the mirrors,
your dad distracted by the football

on his phone. He kisses you to giggles,
we pack our ordinary life into
our ordinary car, drive home
to arguments about bedtime,

hot bath, light sleep,
a Beatrix Potter bedroom,
drawers full of clothes
you still might wear.

Stones

In the afternoons I dream of stones,
their sure shape, the weight of them
in my pockets. I will eat stones. I will
feel grit and sand between my teeth,
I will weigh myself down with stones,
will tie myself down with stones,
will fill the hole in my belly with stones.
My insides will stack like a cairn,
my lungs will be pressed flat like they
are being punished for giving me air.
My stomach will stretch, will burn
to feel their dryness. The stones will line up
in my bowels. My liver will sag beneath
their heft. My uterus will feel grateful
for stones, for anything to fill the void,
for anything to stretch the useless
endometrium. I will weigh myself down
with stones in my pockets, will sew them
into the hem of my skirt, will carry them
in my hands so that I can sink, steady and slow.
I grind my body, like shells to sand
against the stones beneath the sea.

Learning to Cry Quietly

We learn to cry quietly, the grievers of children:
the mothers in their baby's rooms, mocked
by Winnie the Pooh and pastel blankets,
we hide away and weep. Not at first –
at first we scream and wail and gnash our teeth
and beat our fists and break our backs
with stooping, with clinging, with refusing
to let go of clothes and toys, with stamping
their birthdays on the days of the living.

We embrace our grief in restaurants,
in post offices and garden centres, standing
in shops unabashed. But days stack up
to months, and soon the world regrets
to inform you that your grieving time is up.

Two years, three, the ricocheting shrapnel
of a fourth birthday comes only to us, then,
and can't be shared. We learn to cry quietly,
in bathrooms and cars, so they don't ask
when we'll be trying again.

Fuck You

Yes, I'm fat, with a crooked nose
from an accident with a lamppost
and a slightly lazy eye and I look
(or so I'm told) the spitting dab
of my grandmother. I'm thirty-
seven and a bit. I am scarred, I am
scared, I am falling down drunk
on a Saturday night and too hungover
to leave the house. But I run. *You*
see me running, or jogging, or
dragging my fat arse along, puce
in my moon face, eyes watering,
fists clenched, sweating under
each swinging tit, gob gaping
because I'm fat and I am running.
Once upon a time I wore skirts
and bare legs and danced
in clubs and once upon a time
I wore skintight jeans and looked
so hot I set the house on fire. At twenty-
five I could have passed for sixteen
and when that cute little drug habit
kicked in I was the skinniest I've ever been.

And I remember that, like a drunken
dream. Not the stomach in knots
and the fingers down my throat
and the desperation to be thinner,
but the loose hips, lightheaded
high-as-a-kite girl with legs so long
they hurt your eyes and auburn hair
like Anne Boleyn. So, yeah, I've done
my time getting through and fighting on.
Now I am grown up and have a house,
and have a man, and when the things I loved,
I mean, the things I *really* loved, were gone,
despite me being so fucking good, all those
rearview mirror dreams, I fought. I fight on.
This? This training, this getting fitter,
this bringing myself back to something
I half recognise? This is nothing. Not to me.
So go on, laugh it up, turn away, whatever.
I don't give a fuck.